I'm planning my budget, help me to stay
on track by returning this planner to:

_____
INSERT NAME

Greetings,

Thank you for taking that step to purchase this budget planner and tracker. I realize you had many options and chose this one.

This simple budget planner is designed for teens and young adults to acclimate them to the world of financial responsibility.

We all dream of striking an adequately balanced budget that will enable us to indulge in all of life's pleasures like shopping, dining, and travel.

However, it's also true that people budget to gain control over their money so that the lack thereof will not limit the rest of their life!

Budget planning takes dedication, consistency, and patience. However, once you adopt the practice of budgeting, you will eventually start to feel in control of your finances, organized, and able to foresee and advert financial mishaps.

Kinyatta

"YOU MUST GAIN CONTROL OVER YOUR MONEY OR THE LACK OF IT WILL FOREVER CONTROL YOU."

~Dave Ramsey

5 KEY BENEFITS OF CREATING A PERSONAL BUDGET

Budgeting is a necessary and responsible aspect of life that helps you control your spending and stay on track with your financial goals.

At one point in my life, I was a single parent, and I remember writing in a journal every month how much income I expected and my expenses. I recall dreading the 1st of the month since that's when the bulk of my money would be spent. But through writing down my expenses and proper planning, I figured out how to save a little from my second paycheck to lessen the financial strain at the beginning of the month. Unfortunately, many people are just like I used to be – trying to make it from paycheck to paycheck, month to month.

1. **Budgeting helps you to control your spending.**

   When you create a budget, you have a blueprint of how to spend your money. You'll have clarity on all of your income and your expenses and will be able to determine what adjustments to make to avoid being broke!

2. **Budgeting keeps you on track for your financial goals.**

   For example, once I wanted a pair of costly boots. I created a budget and determined how much money per month I'd need to set aside to afford the boots in a specific timeframe. Adding the boots as line items in my budget helped me stay on track to reach my goal. Ahhhh… the reward of budgeting, saving, and then purchasing the boots was sweet!

3. **Budgeting helps you to be less financially overwhelmed.**

   When you budget your money, you know what to expect from month to month, which lessens your stress and anxiety. Planning is the key; writing down all of your expected income and expenses makes a difference. Sometimes you may want to treat yourself to something super special – I'm sure you deserve it. Just add it to your monthly budget so that you're not making a spontaneous purchase that will backfire later.

4. **Budgeting keeps you organized.**

   Disorganization and confusion will stress out the most "Zen" person. While you can't predict the future, you can plan how you will spend your money. Create a space for all of your financial documents and bills. As you pay off your bills, keep all of your receipts and proofs of payment in one place. Here's a story to amplify why this is important. Several years ago, I had a root canal. I didn't pay the bill right away, and the obligation was reported to the credit bureau. I eventually paid the bill and received a receipt, and had it cleared from my credit report. Years later, I returned to the same dentist (yes, the one I took years to pay). When I arrived for my appointment, I remember the snarky nurse telling me I had a balance of $1000 that needed to be paid. After clarifying the balance, I told her I had proof I had already settled the bill. I went home and retrieved my evidence that the bill had been paid in full and went back to the dentist's office. The staff was amazed and a bit taken aback that I indeed had the proof of payment. And yes, I was able to get treated by the dentist. If I had not been organized and saved my receipts and evidence, I'd have been out of luck!

5. **Budgeting sheds light on your spending habits.**

   Be honest when creating your budget. If you're not writing out all of your income and expenses, you're only deceiving yourself. It's essential to understand your spending habits. Many online banking systems offer an analysis of your spending habits based on your credit card usage. It's interesting how much one can spend every day eating out and not realize how much that adds up! It's important to know what your spending habits are and if there are areas in need of improvement. The goal is to strike a balance of meeting your obligations, saving, and being financially flexible.

THE BUDGET CHECKLIST

- [ ] List all of your income and the source (employment, child-support, side-hustle, etc.)
- [ ] List all of your monthly expenses (Yes, even your Victoria Secrets splurges.)
- [ ] Set your goals. Visualize achieving your financial goals.
- [ ] Plan how you will allocate your income based on your goals.
- [ ] Determine if you need to make adjustments to your goals. (This is important because your income may not change so you will need to adjust your goals.)
- [ ] Monitor your budget and stay on track.

7 DAYS OF ABUNDANCE AFFIRMATIONS

SUNDAY
There is always more than enough money in my life.

MONDAY
I am financially free.

TUESDAY
I am financially responsible.

WEDNESDAY
I am a giver and this creates abundance in my life.

THURSDAY
My income exceeds my expenses.

FRIDAY
I attract money.

SATURDAY
I release all resistance to my financial freedom.

MY FINANCIAL VISION BOARD

Add words, images or quotes that represent the financial freedom you envision.

MY FINANCIAL VISION BOARD

Add words, images or quotes that represent the financial freedom you envision.

MY FINANCIAL VISION BOARD

Add words, images or quotes that represent the financial freedom you envision.

30-DAY FINANCIAL FAST

	Today I will refrain from purchasing:	This will save this much money:
1		
2		
3		
4		
5		
6		
7		
8		
9		
10		
11		
12		
13		
14		
15		
16		
17		
18		
19		
20		
21		
22		
23		
24		
25		
26		
27		
28		
29		
30		
31		
	This month I have saved:	

30-DAY FINANCIAL FAST

	Today I will refrain from purchasing:	This will save this much money:
1		
2		
3		
4		
5		
6		
7		
8		
9		
10		
11		
12		
13		
14		
15		
16		
17		
18		
19		
20		
21		
22		
23		
24		
25		
26		
27		
28		
29		
30		
31		
	This month I have saved:	

30-DAY FINANCIAL FAST

	Today I will refrain from purchasing:	This will save this much money:
1		
2		
3		
4		
5		
6		
7		
8		
9		
10		
11		
12		
13		
14		
15		
16		
17		
18		
19		
20		
21		
22		
23		
24		
25		
26		
27		
28		
29		
30		
31		
	This month I have saved:	

30-DAY FINANCIAL FAST

#	Today I will refrain from purchasing:	This will save this much money:
1		
2		
3		
4		
5		
6		
7		
8		
9		
10		
11		
12		
13		
14		
15		
16		
17		
18		
19		
20		
21		
22		
23		
24		
25		
26		
27		
28		
29		
30		
31		
	This month I have saved:	

30-DAY FINANCIAL FAST

#	Today I will refrain from purchasing:	This will save this much money:
1		
2		
3		
4		
5		
6		
7		
8		
9		
10		
11		
12		
13		
14		
15		
16		
17		
18		
19		
20		
21		
22		
23		
24		
25		
26		
27		
28		
29		
30		
31		
	This month I have saved:	

30-DAY FINANCIAL FAST

	Today I will refrain from purchasing:	This will save this much money:
1		
2		
3		
4		
5		
6		
7		
8		
9		
10		
11		
12		
13		
14		
15		
16		
17		
18		
19		
20		
21		
22		
23		
24		
25		
26		
27		
28		
29		
30		
31		
	This month I have saved:	

Monthly Expense Tracker

Housing Expenses	Expected	Actual	Difference
Mortgage/Rent			
Utilities (cable, internet, streaming services)			
HOA Fees			
Renter's Insurance			
Landscaping			
Other:			
Other:			
Other:			
Living Expenses	**Expected**	**Actual**	**Difference**
Food /Groceries			
Childcare			
Care Note/Gas/Insurance			
Clothes/Shoes			
Handbags & Accessories			
Entertainment (movies, concerts, amusement parks, camping)			
Dining out			
Beauty (Hair, Nails, Pedi, Eyebrows)			
Other:			
Other:			
Other:			
Long Term Expenses	**Expected**	**Actual**	**Difference**
New Home fund			
Emergency fund			
Savings fund			
Vacation fund			
Holiday fund			
Wedding fund			
Splurge item fund			
Other:			
Other:			
Other:			

Total Monthly Income:

Total Monthly Expenses:

Savings (difference between expected and actual expenses):

Monthly Expense Tracker

Housing Expenses	Expected	Actual	Difference
Mortgage/Rent			
Utilities (cable, internet, streaming services)			
HOA Fees			
Renter's Insurance			
Landscaping			
Other:			
Other:			
Other:			

Living Expenses	Expected	Actual	Difference
Food /Groceries			
Childcare			
Care Note/Gas/Insurance			
Clothes/Shoes			
Handbags & Accessories			
Entertainment (movies, concerts, amusement parks, camping)			
Dining out			
Beauty (Hair, Nails, Pedi, Eyebrows)			
Other:			
Other:			
Other:			

Long Term Expenses	Expected	Actual	Difference
New Home fund			
Emergency fund			
Savings fund			
Vacation fund			
Holiday fund			
Wedding fund			
Splurge item fund			
Other:			
Other:			
Other:			

Total Monthly Income:

Total Monthly Expenses:

Savings (difference between expected and actual expenses):

Monthly Expense Tracker

Housing Expenses	Expected	Actual	Difference
Mortgage/Rent			
Utilities (cable, internet, streaming services)			
HOA Fees			
Renter's Insurance			
Landscaping			
Other:			
Other:			
Other:			

Living Expenses	Expected	Actual	Difference
Food /Groceries			
Childcare			
Care Note/Gas/Insurance			
Clothes/Shoes			
Handbags & Accessories			
Entertainment (movies, concerts, amusement parks, camping)			
Dining out			
Beauty (Hair, Nails, Pedi, Eyebrows)			
Other:			
Other:			
Other:			

Long Term Expenses	Expected	Actual	Difference
New Home fund			
Emergency fund			
Savings fund			
Vacation fund			
Holiday fund			
Wedding fund			
Splurge item fund			
Other:			
Other:			
Other:			

Total Monthly Income:

Total Monthly Expenses:

Savings (difference between expected and actual expenses):

Monthly Expense Tracker

Housing Expenses	Expected	Actual	Difference
Mortgage/Rent			
Utilities (cable, internet, streaming services)			
HOA Fees			
Renter's Insurance			
Landscaping			
Other:			
Other:			
Other:			
Living Expenses	**Expected**	**Actual**	**Difference**
Food /Groceries			
Childcare			
Care Note/Gas/Insurance			
Clothes/Shoes			
Handbags & Accessories			
Entertainment (movies, concerts, amusement parks, camping)			
Dining out			
Beauty (Hair, Nails, Pedi, Eyebrows)			
Other:			
Other:			
Other:			
Long Term Expenses	**Expected**	**Actual**	**Difference**
New Home fund			
Emergency fund			
Savings fund			
Vacation fund			
Holiday fund			
Wedding fund			
Splurge item fund			
Other:			
Other:			
Other:			

Total Monthly Income:

Total Monthly Expenses:

Savings (difference between expected and actual expenses):

Monthly Expense Tracker

Housing Expenses	Expected	Actual	Difference
Mortgage/Rent			
Utilities (cable, internet, streaming services)			
HOA Fees			
Renter's Insurance			
Landscaping			
Other:			
Other:			
Other:			

Living Expenses	Expected	Actual	Difference
Food /Groceries			
Childcare			
Care Note/Gas/Insurance			
Clothes/Shoes			
Handbags & Accessories			
Entertainment (movies, concerts, amusement parks, camping)			
Dining out			
Beauty (Hair, Nails, Pedi, Eyebrows)			
Other:			
Other:			
Other:			

Long Term Expenses	Expected	Actual	Difference
New Home fund			
Emergency fund			
Savings fund			
Vacation fund			
Holiday fund			
Wedding fund			
Splurge item fund			
Other:			
Other:			
Other:			

Total Monthly Income:

Total Monthly Expenses:

Savings (difference between expected and actual expenses):

Monthly Expense Tracker

Housing Expenses	Expected	Actual	Difference
Mortgage/Rent			
Utilities (cable, internet, streaming services)			
HOA Fees			
Renter's Insurance			
Landscaping			
Other:			
Other:			
Other:			

Living Expenses	Expected	Actual	Difference
Food /Groceries			
Childcare			
Care Note/Gas/Insurance			
Clothes/Shoes			
Handbags & Accessories			
Entertainment (movies, concerts, amusement parks, camping)			
Dining out			
Beauty (Hair, Nails, Pedi, Eyebrows)			
Other:			
Other:			
Other:			

Long Term Expenses	Expected	Actual	Difference
New Home fund			
Emergency fund			
Savings fund			
Vacation fund			
Holiday fund			
Wedding fund			
Splurge item fund			
Other:			
Other:			
Other:			

Total Monthly Income:

Total Monthly Expenses:

Savings (difference between expected and actual expenses):

Monthly Expense Tracker

Housing Expenses	Expected	Actual	Difference
Mortgage/Rent			
Utilities (cable, internet, streaming services)			
HOA Fees			
Renter's Insurance			
Landscaping			
Other:			
Other:			
Other:			
Living Expenses	**Expected**	**Actual**	**Difference**
Food /Groceries			
Childcare			
Care Note/Gas/Insurance			
Clothes/Shoes			
Handbags & Accessories			
Entertainment (movies, concerts, amusement parks, camping)			
Dining out			
Beauty (Hair, Nails, Pedi, Eyebrows)			
Other:			
Other:			
Other:			
Long Term Expenses	**Expected**	**Actual**	**Difference**
New Home fund			
Emergency fund			
Savings fund			
Vacation fund			
Holiday fund			
Wedding fund			
Splurge item fund			
Other:			
Other:			
Other:			

Total Monthly Income:

Total Monthly Expenses:

Savings (difference between expected and actual expenses):

Monthly Expense Tracker

Housing Expenses	Expected	Actual	Difference
Mortgage/Rent			
Utilities (cable, internet, streaming services)			
HOA Fees			
Renter's Insurance			
Landscaping			
Other:			
Other:			
Other:			
Living Expenses	**Expected**	**Actual**	**Difference**
Food /Groceries			
Childcare			
Care Note/Gas/Insurance			
Clothes/Shoes			
Handbags & Accessories			
Entertainment (movies, concerts, amusement parks, camping)			
Dining out			
Beauty (Hair, Nails, Pedi, Eyebrows)			
Other:			
Other:			
Other:			
Long Term Expenses	**Expected**	**Actual**	**Difference**
New Home fund			
Emergency fund			
Savings fund			
Vacation fund			
Holiday fund			
Wedding fund			
Splurge item fund			
Other:			
Other:			
Other:			

Total Monthly Income:

Total Monthly Expenses:

Savings (difference between expected and actual expenses):

Monthly Expense Tracker

Housing Expenses	Expected	Actual	Difference
Mortgage/Rent			
Utilities (cable, internet, streaming services)			
HOA Fees			
Renter's Insurance			
Landscaping			
Other:			
Other:			
Other:			

Living Expenses	Expected	Actual	Difference
Food /Groceries			
Childcare			
Care Note/Gas/Insurance			
Clothes/Shoes			
Handbags & Accessories			
Entertainment (movies, concerts, amusement parks, camping)			
Dining out			
Beauty (Hair, Nails, Pedi, Eyebrows)			
Other:			
Other:			
Other:			

Long Term Expenses	Expected	Actual	Difference
New Home fund			
Emergency fund			
Savings fund			
Vacation fund			
Holiday fund			
Wedding fund			
Splurge item fund			
Other:			
Other:			
Other:			

Total Monthly Income:

Total Monthly Expenses:

Savings (difference between expected and actual expenses):

Monthly Expense Tracker

Housing Expenses	Expected	Actual	Difference
Mortgage/Rent			
Utilities (cable, internet, streaming services)			
HOA Fees			
Renter's Insurance			
Landscaping			
Other:			
Other:			
Other:			

Living Expenses	Expected	Actual	Difference
Food /Groceries			
Childcare			
Care Note/Gas/Insurance			
Clothes/Shoes			
Handbags & Accessories			
Entertainment (movies, concerts, amusement parks, camping)			
Dining out			
Beauty (Hair, Nails, Pedi, Eyebrows)			
Other:			
Other:			
Other:			

Long Term Expenses	Expected	Actual	Difference
New Home fund			
Emergency fund			
Savings fund			
Vacation fund			
Holiday fund			
Wedding fund			
Splurge item fund			
Other:			
Other:			
Other:			

Total Monthly Income:

Total Monthly Expenses:

Savings (difference between expected and actual expenses):

Monthly Expense Tracker

Housing Expenses	Expected	Actual	Difference
Mortgage/Rent			
Utilities (cable, internet, streaming services)			
HOA Fees			
Renter's Insurance			
Landscaping			
Other:			
Other:			
Other:			

Living Expenses	Expected	Actual	Difference
Food /Groceries			
Childcare			
Care Note/Gas/Insurance			
Clothes/Shoes			
Handbags & Accessories			
Entertainment (movies, concerts, amusement parks, camping)			
Dining out			
Beauty (Hair, Nails, Pedi, Eyebrows)			
Other:			
Other:			
Other:			

Long Term Expenses	Expected	Actual	Difference
New Home fund			
Emergency fund			
Savings fund			
Vacation fund			
Holiday fund			
Wedding fund			
Splurge item fund			
Other:			
Other:			
Other:			

Total Monthly Income:

Total Monthly Expenses:

Savings (difference between expected and actual expenses):

Monthly Expense Tracker

Housing Expenses	Expected	Actual	Difference
Mortgage/Rent			
Utilities (cable, internet, streaming services)			
HOA Fees			
Renter's Insurance			
Landscaping			
Other:			
Other:			
Other:			

Living Expenses	Expected	Actual	Difference
Food /Groceries			
Childcare			
Care Note/Gas/Insurance			
Clothes/Shoes			
Handbags & Accessories			
Entertainment (movies, concerts, amusement parks, camping)			
Dining out			
Beauty (Hair, Nails, Pedi, Eyebrows)			
Other:			
Other:			
Other:			

Long Term Expenses	Expected	Actual	Difference
New Home fund			
Emergency fund			
Savings fund			
Vacation fund			
Holiday fund			
Wedding fund			
Splurge item fund			
Other:			
Other:			
Other:			

Total Monthly Income:

Total Monthly Expenses:

Savings (difference between expected and actual expenses):

Monthly Expense Tracker

Housing Expenses	Expected	Actual	Difference
Mortgage/Rent			
Utilities (cable, internet, streaming services)			
HOA Fees			
Renter's Insurance			
Landscaping			
Other:			
Other:			
Other:			

Living Expenses	Expected	Actual	Difference
Food /Groceries			
Childcare			
Care Note/Gas/Insurance			
Clothes/Shoes			
Handbags & Accessories			
Entertainment (movies, concerts, amusement parks, camping)			
Dining out			
Beauty (Hair, Nails, Pedi, Eyebrows)			
Other:			
Other:			
Other:			

Long Term Expenses	Expected	Actual	Difference
New Home fund			
Emergency fund			
Savings fund			
Vacation fund			
Holiday fund			
Wedding fund			
Splurge item fund			
Other:			
Other:			
Other:			

Total Monthly Income:

Total Monthly Expenses:

Savings (difference between expected and actual expenses):

Monthly Expense Tracker

Housing Expenses	Expected	Actual	Difference
Mortgage/Rent			
Utilities (cable, internet, streaming services)			
HOA Fees			
Renter's Insurance			
Landscaping			
Other:			
Other:			
Other:			

Living Expenses	Expected	Actual	Difference
Food /Groceries			
Childcare			
Care Note/Gas/Insurance			
Clothes/Shoes			
Handbags & Accessories			
Entertainment (movies, concerts, amusement parks, camping)			
Dining out			
Beauty (Hair, Nails, Pedi, Eyebrows)			
Other:			
Other:			
Other:			

Long Term Expenses	Expected	Actual	Difference
New Home fund			
Emergency fund			
Savings fund			
Vacation fund			
Holiday fund			
Wedding fund			
Splurge item fund			
Other:			
Other:			
Other:			

Total Monthly Income:

Total Monthly Expenses:

Savings (difference between expected and actual expenses):

Monthly Expense Tracker

Housing Expenses	Expected	Actual	Difference
Mortgage/Rent			
Utilities (cable, internet, streaming services)			
HOA Fees			
Renter's Insurance			
Landscaping			
Other:			
Other:			
Other:			

Living Expenses	Expected	Actual	Difference
Food /Groceries			
Childcare			
Care Note/Gas/Insurance			
Clothes/Shoes			
Handbags & Accessories			
Entertainment (movies, concerts, amusement parks, camping)			
Dining out			
Beauty (Hair, Nails, Pedi, Eyebrows)			
Other:			
Other:			
Other:			

Long Term Expenses	Expected	Actual	Difference
New Home fund			
Emergency fund			
Savings fund			
Vacation fund			
Holiday fund			
Wedding fund			
Splurge item fund			
Other:			
Other:			
Other:			

Total Monthly Income:

Total Monthly Expenses:

Savings (difference between expected and actual expenses):

Monthly Expense Tracker

Housing Expenses	Expected	Actual	Difference
Mortgage/Rent			
Utilities (cable, internet, streaming services)			
HOA Fees			
Renter's Insurance			
Landscaping			
Other:			
Other:			
Other:			

Living Expenses	Expected	Actual	Difference
Food /Groceries			
Childcare			
Care Note/Gas/Insurance			
Clothes/Shoes			
Handbags & Accessories			
Entertainment (movies, concerts, amusement parks, camping)			
Dining out			
Beauty (Hair, Nails, Pedi, Eyebrows)			
Other:			
Other:			
Other:			

Long Term Expenses	Expected	Actual	Difference
New Home fund			
Emergency fund			
Savings fund			
Vacation fund			
Holiday fund			
Wedding fund			
Splurge item fund			
Other:			
Other:			
Other:			

Total Monthly Income:

Total Monthly Expenses:

Savings (difference between expected and actual expenses):

Monthly Expense Tracker

Housing Expenses	Expected	Actual	Difference
Mortgage/Rent			
Utilities (cable, internet, streaming services)			
HOA Fees			
Renter's Insurance			
Landscaping			
Other:			
Other:			
Other:			

Living Expenses	Expected	Actual	Difference
Food /Groceries			
Childcare			
Care Note/Gas/Insurance			
Clothes/Shoes			
Handbags & Accessories			
Entertainment (movies, concerts, amusement parks, camping)			
Dining out			
Beauty (Hair, Nails, Pedi, Eyebrows)			
Other:			
Other:			
Other:			

Long Term Expenses	Expected	Actual	Difference
New Home fund			
Emergency fund			
Savings fund			
Vacation fund			
Holiday fund			
Wedding fund			
Splurge item fund			
Other:			
Other:			
Other:			

Total Monthly Income:

Total Monthly Expenses:

Savings (difference between expected and actual expenses):

Monthly Expense Tracker

Housing Expenses	Expected	Actual	Difference
Mortgage/Rent			
Utilities (cable, internet, streaming services)			
HOA Fees			
Renter's Insurance			
Landscaping			
Other:			
Other:			
Other:			
Living Expenses	**Expected**	**Actual**	**Difference**
Food /Groceries			
Childcare			
Care Note/Gas/Insurance			
Clothes/Shoes			
Handbags & Accessories			
Entertainment (movies, concerts, amusement parks, camping)			
Dining out			
Beauty (Hair, Nails, Pedi, Eyebrows)			
Other:			
Other:			
Other:			
Long Term Expenses	**Expected**	**Actual**	**Difference**
New Home fund			
Emergency fund			
Savings fund			
Vacation fund			
Holiday fund			
Wedding fund			
Splurge item fund			
Other:			
Other:			
Other:			

Total Monthly Income:

Total Monthly Expenses:

Savings (difference between expected and actual expenses):

Monthly Expense Tracker

Housing Expenses	Expected	Actual	Difference
Mortgage/Rent			
Utilities (cable, internet, streaming services)			
HOA Fees			
Renter's Insurance			
Landscaping			
Other:			
Other:			
Other:			

Living Expenses	Expected	Actual	Difference
Food /Groceries			
Childcare			
Care Note/Gas/Insurance			
Clothes/Shoes			
Handbags & Accessories			
Entertainment (movies, concerts, amusement parks, camping)			
Dining out			
Beauty (Hair, Nails, Pedi, Eyebrows)			
Other:			
Other:			
Other:			

Long Term Expenses	Expected	Actual	Difference
New Home fund			
Emergency fund			
Savings fund			
Vacation fund			
Holiday fund			
Wedding fund			
Splurge item fund			
Other:			
Other:			
Other:			

Total Monthly Income:

Total Monthly Expenses:

Savings (difference between expected and actual expenses):

Monthly Expense Tracker

Housing Expenses	Expected	Actual	Difference
Mortgage/Rent			
Utilities (cable, internet, streaming services)			
HOA Fees			
Renter's Insurance			
Landscaping			
Other:			
Other:			
Other:			

Living Expenses	Expected	Actual	Difference
Food /Groceries			
Childcare			
Care Note/Gas/Insurance			
Clothes/Shoes			
Handbags & Accessories			
Entertainment (movies, concerts, amusement parks, camping)			
Dining out			
Beauty (Hair, Nails, Pedi, Eyebrows)			
Other:			
Other:			
Other:			

Long Term Expenses	Expected	Actual	Difference
New Home fund			
Emergency fund			
Savings fund			
Vacation fund			
Holiday fund			
Wedding fund			
Splurge item fund			
Other:			
Other:			
Other:			

Total Monthly Income:

Total Monthly Expenses:

Savings (difference between expected and actual expenses):

Monthly Expense Tracker

Housing Expenses	Expected	Actual	Difference
Mortgage/Rent			
Utilities (cable, internet, streaming services)			
HOA Fees			
Renter's Insurance			
Landscaping			
Other:			
Other:			
Other:			
Living Expenses	**Expected**	**Actual**	**Difference**
Food /Groceries			
Childcare			
Care Note/Gas/Insurance			
Clothes/Shoes			
Handbags & Accessories			
Entertainment (movies, concerts, amusement parks, camping)			
Dining out			
Beauty (Hair, Nails, Pedi, Eyebrows)			
Other:			
Other:			
Other:			
Long Term Expenses	**Expected**	**Actual**	**Difference**
New Home fund			
Emergency fund			
Savings fund			
Vacation fund			
Holiday fund			
Wedding fund			
Splurge item fund			
Other:			
Other:			
Other:			

Total Monthly Income:

Total Monthly Expenses:

Savings (difference between expected and actual expenses):

Monthly Expense Tracker

Housing Expenses	Expected	Actual	Difference
Mortgage/Rent			
Utilities (cable, internet, streaming services)			
HOA Fees			
Renter's Insurance			
Landscaping			
Other:			
Other:			
Other:			

Living Expenses	Expected	Actual	Difference
Food /Groceries			
Childcare			
Care Note/Gas/Insurance			
Clothes/Shoes			
Handbags & Accessories			
Entertainment (movies, concerts, amusement parks, camping)			
Dining out			
Beauty (Hair, Nails, Pedi, Eyebrows)			
Other:			
Other:			
Other:			

Long Term Expenses	Expected	Actual	Difference
New Home fund			
Emergency fund			
Savings fund			
Vacation fund			
Holiday fund			
Wedding fund			
Splurge item fund			
Other:			
Other:			
Other:			

Total Monthly Income:

Total Monthly Expenses:

Savings (difference between expected and actual expenses):

Monthly Expense Tracker

Housing Expenses	Expected	Actual	Difference
Mortgage/Rent			
Utilities (cable, internet, streaming services)			
HOA Fees			
Renter's Insurance			
Landscaping			
Other:			
Other:			
Other:			

Living Expenses	Expected	Actual	Difference
Food /Groceries			
Childcare			
Care Note/Gas/Insurance			
Clothes/Shoes			
Handbags & Accessories			
Entertainment (movies, concerts, amusement parks, camping)			
Dining out			
Beauty (Hair, Nails, Pedi, Eyebrows)			
Other:			
Other:			
Other:			

Long Term Expenses	Expected	Actual	Difference
New Home fund			
Emergency fund			
Savings fund			
Vacation fund			
Holiday fund			
Wedding fund			
Splurge item fund			
Other:			
Other:			
Other:			

Total Monthly Income:

Total Monthly Expenses:

Savings (difference between expected and actual expenses):

Monthly Expense Tracker

Housing Expenses	Expected	Actual	Difference
Mortgage/Rent			
Utilities (cable, internet, streaming services)			
HOA Fees			
Renter's Insurance			
Landscaping			
Other:			
Other:			
Other:			

Living Expenses	Expected	Actual	Difference
Food /Groceries			
Childcare			
Care Note/Gas/Insurance			
Clothes/Shoes			
Handbags & Accessories			
Entertainment (movies, concerts, amusement parks, camping)			
Dining out			
Beauty (Hair, Nails, Pedi, Eyebrows)			
Other:			
Other:			
Other:			

Long Term Expenses	Expected	Actual	Difference
New Home fund			
Emergency fund			
Savings fund			
Vacation fund			
Holiday fund			
Wedding fund			
Splurge item fund			
Other:			
Other:			
Other:			

Total Monthly Income:

Total Monthly Expenses:

Savings (difference between expected and actual expenses):

Monthly Expense Tracker

Housing Expenses	Expected	Actual	Difference
Mortgage/Rent			
Utilities (cable, internet, streaming services)			
HOA Fees			
Renter's Insurance			
Landscaping			
Other:			
Other:			
Other:			

Living Expenses	Expected	Actual	Difference
Food /Groceries			
Childcare			
Care Note/Gas/Insurance			
Clothes/Shoes			
Handbags & Accessories			
Entertainment (movies, concerts, amusement parks, camping)			
Dining out			
Beauty (Hair, Nails, Pedi, Eyebrows)			
Other:			
Other:			
Other:			

Long Term Expenses	Expected	Actual	Difference
New Home fund			
Emergency fund			
Savings fund			
Vacation fund			
Holiday fund			
Wedding fund			
Splurge item fund			
Other:			
Other:			
Other:			

Total Monthly Income:

Total Monthly Expenses:

Savings (difference between expected and actual expenses):

Monthly Expense Tracker

Housing Expenses	Expected	Actual	Difference
Mortgage/Rent			
Utilities (cable, internet, streaming services)			
HOA Fees			
Renter's Insurance			
Landscaping			
Other:			
Other:			
Other:			

Living Expenses	Expected	Actual	Difference
Food /Groceries			
Childcare			
Care Note/Gas/Insurance			
Clothes/Shoes			
Handbags & Accessories			
Entertainment (movies, concerts, amusement parks, camping)			
Dining out			
Beauty (Hair, Nails, Pedi, Eyebrows)			
Other:			
Other:			
Other:			

Long Term Expenses	Expected	Actual	Difference
New Home fund			
Emergency fund			
Savings fund			
Vacation fund			
Holiday fund			
Wedding fund			
Splurge item fund			
Other:			
Other:			
Other:			

Total Monthly Income:

Total Monthly Expenses:

Savings (difference between expected and actual expenses):

Monthly Expense Tracker

Housing Expenses	Expected	Actual	Difference
Mortgage/Rent			
Utilities (cable, internet, streaming services)			
HOA Fees			
Renter's Insurance			
Landscaping			
Other:			
Other:			
Other:			

Living Expenses	Expected	Actual	Difference
Food /Groceries			
Childcare			
Care Note/Gas/Insurance			
Clothes/Shoes			
Handbags & Accessories			
Entertainment (movies, concerts, amusement parks, camping)			
Dining out			
Beauty (Hair, Nails, Pedi, Eyebrows)			
Other:			
Other:			
Other:			

Long Term Expenses	Expected	Actual	Difference
New Home fund			
Emergency fund			
Savings fund			
Vacation fund			
Holiday fund			
Wedding fund			
Splurge item fund			
Other:			
Other:			
Other:			

Total Monthly Income:

Total Monthly Expenses:

Savings (difference between expected and actual expenses):

Monthly Expense Tracker

Housing Expenses	Expected	Actual	Difference
Mortgage/Rent			
Utilities (cable, internet, streaming services)			
HOA Fees			
Renter's Insurance			
Landscaping			
Other:			
Other:			
Other:			

Living Expenses	Expected	Actual	Difference
Food /Groceries			
Childcare			
Care Note/Gas/Insurance			
Clothes/Shoes			
Handbags & Accessories			
Entertainment (movies, concerts, amusement parks, camping)			
Dining out			
Beauty (Hair, Nails, Pedi, Eyebrows)			
Other:			
Other:			
Other:			

Long Term Expenses	Expected	Actual	Difference
New Home fund			
Emergency fund			
Savings fund			
Vacation fund			
Holiday fund			
Wedding fund			
Splurge item fund			
Other:			
Other:			
Other:			

Total Monthly Income:

Total Monthly Expenses:

Savings (difference between expected and actual expenses):

Monthly Expense Tracker

Housing Expenses	Expected	Actual	Difference
Mortgage/Rent			
Utilities (cable, internet, streaming services)			
HOA Fees			
Renter's Insurance			
Landscaping			
Other:			
Other:			
Other:			
Living Expenses	**Expected**	**Actual**	**Difference**
Food /Groceries			
Childcare			
Care Note/Gas/Insurance			
Clothes/Shoes			
Handbags & Accessories			
Entertainment (movies, concerts, amusement parks, camping)			
Dining out			
Beauty (Hair, Nails, Pedi, Eyebrows)			
Other:			
Other:			
Other:			
Long Term Expenses	**Expected**	**Actual**	**Difference**
New Home fund			
Emergency fund			
Savings fund			
Vacation fund			
Holiday fund			
Wedding fund			
Splurge item fund			
Other:			
Other:			
Other:			

Total Monthly Income:

Total Monthly Expenses:

Savings (difference between expected and actual expenses):

Monthly Expense Tracker

Housing Expenses	Expected	Actual	Difference
Mortgage/Rent			
Utilities (cable, internet, streaming services)			
HOA Fees			
Renter's Insurance			
Landscaping			
Other:			
Other:			
Other:			
Living Expenses	**Expected**	**Actual**	**Difference**
Food /Groceries			
Childcare			
Care Note/Gas/Insurance			
Clothes/Shoes			
Handbags & Accessories			
Entertainment (movies, concerts, amusement parks, camping)			
Dining out			
Beauty (Hair, Nails, Pedi, Eyebrows)			
Other:			
Other:			
Other:			
Long Term Expenses	**Expected**	**Actual**	**Difference**
New Home fund			
Emergency fund			
Savings fund			
Vacation fund			
Holiday fund			
Wedding fund			
Splurge item fund			
Other:			
Other:			
Other:			

Total Monthly Income:

Total Monthly Expenses:

Savings (difference between expected and actual expenses):

Monthly Expense Tracker

Housing Expenses	Expected	Actual	Difference
Mortgage/Rent			
Utilities (cable, internet, streaming services)			
HOA Fees			
Renter's Insurance			
Landscaping			
Other:			
Other:			
Other:			

Living Expenses	Expected	Actual	Difference
Food /Groceries			
Childcare			
Care Note/Gas/Insurance			
Clothes/Shoes			
Handbags & Accessories			
Entertainment (movies, concerts, amusement parks, camping)			
Dining out			
Beauty (Hair, Nails, Pedi, Eyebrows)			
Other:			
Other:			
Other:			

Long Term Expenses	Expected	Actual	Difference
New Home fund			
Emergency fund			
Savings fund			
Vacation fund			
Holiday fund			
Wedding fund			
Splurge item fund			
Other:			
Other:			
Other:			

Total Monthly Income:

Total Monthly Expenses:

Savings (difference between expected and actual expenses):

Monthly Expense Tracker

Housing Expenses	Expected	Actual	Difference
Mortgage/Rent			
Utilities (cable, internet, streaming services)			
HOA Fees			
Renter's Insurance			
Landscaping			
Other:			
Other:			
Other:			

Living Expenses	Expected	Actual	Difference
Food /Groceries			
Childcare			
Care Note/Gas/Insurance			
Clothes/Shoes			
Handbags & Accessories			
Entertainment (movies, concerts, amusement parks, camping)			
Dining out			
Beauty (Hair, Nails, Pedi, Eyebrows)			
Other:			
Other:			
Other:			

Long Term Expenses	Expected	Actual	Difference
New Home fund			
Emergency fund			
Savings fund			
Vacation fund			
Holiday fund			
Wedding fund			
Splurge item fund			
Other:			
Other:			
Other:			

Total Monthly Income:

Total Monthly Expenses:

Savings (difference between expected and actual expenses):

Monthly Expense Tracker

Housing Expenses	Expected	Actual	Difference
Mortgage/Rent			
Utilities (cable, internet, streaming services)			
HOA Fees			
Renter's Insurance			
Landscaping			
Other:			
Other:			
Other:			

Living Expenses	Expected	Actual	Difference
Food /Groceries			
Childcare			
Care Note/Gas/Insurance			
Clothes/Shoes			
Handbags & Accessories			
Entertainment (movies, concerts, amusement parks, camping)			
Dining out			
Beauty (Hair, Nails, Pedi, Eyebrows)			
Other:			
Other:			
Other:			

Long Term Expenses	Expected	Actual	Difference
New Home fund			
Emergency fund			
Savings fund			
Vacation fund			
Holiday fund			
Wedding fund			
Splurge item fund			
Other:			
Other:			
Other:			

Total Monthly Income:

Total Monthly Expenses:

Savings (difference between expected and actual expenses):

Monthly Expense Tracker

Housing Expenses	Expected	Actual	Difference
Mortgage/Rent			
Utilities (cable, internet, streaming services)			
HOA Fees			
Renter's Insurance			
Landscaping			
Other:			
Other:			
Other:			

Living Expenses	Expected	Actual	Difference
Food /Groceries			
Childcare			
Care Note/Gas/Insurance			
Clothes/Shoes			
Handbags & Accessories			
Entertainment (movies, concerts, amusement parks, camping)			
Dining out			
Beauty (Hair, Nails, Pedi, Eyebrows)			
Other:			
Other:			
Other:			

Long Term Expenses	Expected	Actual	Difference
New Home fund			
Emergency fund			
Savings fund			
Vacation fund			
Holiday fund			
Wedding fund			
Splurge item fund			
Other:			
Other:			
Other:			

Total Monthly Income:

Total Monthly Expenses:

Savings (difference between expected and actual expenses):

Monthly Expense Tracker

Housing Expenses	Expected	Actual	Difference
Mortgage/Rent			
Utilities (cable, internet, streaming services)			
HOA Fees			
Renter's Insurance			
Landscaping			
Other:			
Other:			
Other:			

Living Expenses	Expected	Actual	Difference
Food /Groceries			
Childcare			
Care Note/Gas/Insurance			
Clothes/Shoes			
Handbags & Accessories			
Entertainment (movies, concerts, amusement parks, camping)			
Dining out			
Beauty (Hair, Nails, Pedi, Eyebrows)			
Other:			
Other:			
Other:			

Long Term Expenses	Expected	Actual	Difference
New Home fund			
Emergency fund			
Savings fund			
Vacation fund			
Holiday fund			
Wedding fund			
Splurge item fund			
Other:			
Other:			
Other:			

Total Monthly Income:

Total Monthly Expenses:

Savings (difference between expected and actual expenses):

Monthly Expense Tracker

Housing Expenses	Expected	Actual	Difference
Mortgage/Rent			
Utilities (cable, internet, streaming services)			
HOA Fees			
Renter's Insurance			
Landscaping			
Other:			
Other:			
Other:			
Living Expenses	**Expected**	**Actual**	**Difference**
Food /Groceries			
Childcare			
Care Note/Gas/Insurance			
Clothes/Shoes			
Handbags & Accessories			
Entertainment (movies, concerts, amusement parks, camping)			
Dining out			
Beauty (Hair, Nails, Pedi, Eyebrows)			
Other:			
Other:			
Other:			
Long Term Expenses	**Expected**	**Actual**	**Difference**
New Home fund			
Emergency fund			
Savings fund			
Vacation fund			
Holiday fund			
Wedding fund			
Splurge item fund			
Other:			
Other:			
Other:			

Total Monthly Income:

Total Monthly Expenses:

Savings (difference between expected and actual expenses):

Monthly Expense Tracker

Housing Expenses	Expected	Actual	Difference
Mortgage/Rent			
Utilities (cable, internet, streaming services)			
HOA Fees			
Renter's Insurance			
Landscaping			
Other:			
Other:			
Other:			

Living Expenses	Expected	Actual	Difference
Food /Groceries			
Childcare			
Care Note/Gas/Insurance			
Clothes/Shoes			
Handbags & Accessories			
Entertainment (movies, concerts, amusement parks, camping)			
Dining out			
Beauty (Hair, Nails, Pedi, Eyebrows)			
Other:			
Other:			
Other:			

Long Term Expenses	Expected	Actual	Difference
New Home fund			
Emergency fund			
Savings fund			
Vacation fund			
Holiday fund			
Wedding fund			
Splurge item fund			
Other:			
Other:			
Other:			

Total Monthly Income:

Total Monthly Expenses:

Savings (difference between expected and actual expenses):

Monthly Expense Tracker

Housing Expenses	Expected	Actual	Difference
Mortgage/Rent			
Utilities (cable, internet, streaming services)			
HOA Fees			
Renter's Insurance			
Landscaping			
Other:			
Other:			
Other:			

Living Expenses	Expected	Actual	Difference
Food /Groceries			
Childcare			
Care Note/Gas/Insurance			
Clothes/Shoes			
Handbags & Accessories			
Entertainment (movies, concerts, amusement parks, camping)			
Dining out			
Beauty (Hair, Nails, Pedi, Eyebrows)			
Other:			
Other:			
Other:			

Long Term Expenses	Expected	Actual	Difference
New Home fund			
Emergency fund			
Savings fund			
Vacation fund			
Holiday fund			
Wedding fund			
Splurge item fund			
Other:			
Other:			
Other:			

Total Monthly Income:

Total Monthly Expenses:

Savings (difference between expected and actual expenses):

Monthly Expense Tracker

Housing Expenses	Expected	Actual	Difference
Mortgage/Rent			
Utilities (cable, internet, streaming services)			
HOA Fees			
Renter's Insurance			
Landscaping			
Other:			
Other:			
Other:			

Living Expenses	Expected	Actual	Difference
Food /Groceries			
Childcare			
Care Note/Gas/Insurance			
Clothes/Shoes			
Handbags & Accessories			
Entertainment (movies, concerts, amusement parks, camping)			
Dining out			
Beauty (Hair, Nails, Pedi, Eyebrows)			
Other:			
Other:			
Other:			

Long Term Expenses	Expected	Actual	Difference
New Home fund			
Emergency fund			
Savings fund			
Vacation fund			
Holiday fund			
Wedding fund			
Splurge item fund			
Other:			
Other:			
Other:			

Total Monthly Income:

Total Monthly Expenses:

Savings (difference between expected and actual expenses):

Monthly Expense Tracker

Housing Expenses	Expected	Actual	Difference
Mortgage/Rent			
Utilities (cable, internet, streaming services)			
HOA Fees			
Renter's Insurance			
Landscaping			
Other:			
Other:			
Other:			

Living Expenses	Expected	Actual	Difference
Food /Groceries			
Childcare			
Care Note/Gas/Insurance			
Clothes/Shoes			
Handbags & Accessories			
Entertainment (movies, concerts, amusement parks, camping)			
Dining out			
Beauty (Hair, Nails, Pedi, Eyebrows)			
Other:			
Other:			
Other:			

Long Term Expenses	Expected	Actual	Difference
New Home fund			
Emergency fund			
Savings fund			
Vacation fund			
Holiday fund			
Wedding fund			
Splurge item fund			
Other:			
Other:			
Other:			

Total Monthly Income:

Total Monthly Expenses:

Savings (difference between expected and actual expenses):

Monthly Expense Tracker

Housing Expenses	Expected	Actual	Difference
Mortgage/Rent			
Utilities (cable, internet, streaming services)			
HOA Fees			
Renter's Insurance			
Landscaping			
Other:			
Other:			
Other:			

Living Expenses	Expected	Actual	Difference
Food /Groceries			
Childcare			
Care Note/Gas/Insurance			
Clothes/Shoes			
Handbags & Accessories			
Entertainment (movies, concerts, amusement parks, camping)			
Dining out			
Beauty (Hair, Nails, Pedi, Eyebrows)			
Other:			
Other:			
Other:			

Long Term Expenses	Expected	Actual	Difference
New Home fund			
Emergency fund			
Savings fund			
Vacation fund			
Holiday fund			
Wedding fund			
Splurge item fund			
Other:			
Other:			
Other:			

Total Monthly Income:

Total Monthly Expenses:

Savings (difference between expected and actual expenses):

Monthly Expense Tracker

Housing Expenses	Expected	Actual	Difference
Mortgage/Rent			
Utilities (cable, internet, streaming services)			
HOA Fees			
Renter's Insurance			
Landscaping			
Other:			
Other:			
Other:			

Living Expenses	Expected	Actual	Difference
Food /Groceries			
Childcare			
Care Note/Gas/Insurance			
Clothes/Shoes			
Handbags & Accessories			
Entertainment (movies, concerts, amusement parks, camping)			
Dining out			
Beauty (Hair, Nails, Pedi, Eyebrows)			
Other:			
Other:			
Other:			

Long Term Expenses	Expected	Actual	Difference
New Home fund			
Emergency fund			
Savings fund			
Vacation fund			
Holiday fund			
Wedding fund			
Splurge item fund			
Other:			
Other:			
Other:			

Total Monthly Income:

Total Monthly Expenses:

Savings (difference between expected and actual expenses):

Monthly Expense Tracker

Housing Expenses	Expected	Actual	Difference
Mortgage/Rent			
Utilities (cable, internet, streaming services)			
HOA Fees			
Renter's Insurance			
Landscaping			
Other:			
Other:			
Other:			

Living Expenses	Expected	Actual	Difference
Food /Groceries			
Childcare			
Care Note/Gas/Insurance			
Clothes/Shoes			
Handbags & Accessories			
Entertainment (movies, concerts, amusement parks, camping)			
Dining out			
Beauty (Hair, Nails, Pedi, Eyebrows)			
Other:			
Other:			
Other:			

Long Term Expenses	Expected	Actual	Difference
New Home fund			
Emergency fund			
Savings fund			
Vacation fund			
Holiday fund			
Wedding fund			
Splurge item fund			
Other:			
Other:			
Other:			

Total Monthly Income:

Total Monthly Expenses:

Savings (difference between expected and actual expenses):

Monthly Expense Tracker

Housing Expenses	Expected	Actual	Difference
Mortgage/Rent			
Utilities (cable, internet, streaming services)			
HOA Fees			
Renter's Insurance			
Landscaping			
Other:			
Other:			
Other:			

Living Expenses	Expected	Actual	Difference
Food /Groceries			
Childcare			
Care Note/Gas/Insurance			
Clothes/Shoes			
Handbags & Accessories			
Entertainment (movies, concerts, amusement parks, camping)			
Dining out			
Beauty (Hair, Nails, Pedi, Eyebrows)			
Other:			
Other:			
Other:			

Long Term Expenses	Expected	Actual	Difference
New Home fund			
Emergency fund			
Savings fund			
Vacation fund			
Holiday fund			
Wedding fund			
Splurge item fund			
Other:			
Other:			
Other:			

Total Monthly Income:

Total Monthly Expenses:

Savings (difference between expected and actual expenses):

Monthly Expense Tracker

Housing Expenses	Expected	Actual	Difference
Mortgage/Rent			
Utilities (cable, internet, streaming services)			
HOA Fees			
Renter's Insurance			
Landscaping			
Other:			
Other:			
Other:			

Living Expenses	Expected	Actual	Difference
Food /Groceries			
Childcare			
Care Note/Gas/Insurance			
Clothes/Shoes			
Handbags & Accessories			
Entertainment (movies, concerts, amusement parks, camping)			
Dining out			
Beauty (Hair, Nails, Pedi, Eyebrows)			
Other:			
Other:			
Other:			

Long Term Expenses	Expected	Actual	Difference
New Home fund			
Emergency fund			
Savings fund			
Vacation fund			
Holiday fund			
Wedding fund			
Splurge item fund			
Other:			
Other:			
Other:			

Total Monthly Income:

Total Monthly Expenses:

Savings (difference between expected and actual expenses):

Monthly Expense Tracker

Housing Expenses	Expected	Actual	Difference
Mortgage/Rent			
Utilities (cable, internet, streaming services)			
HOA Fees			
Renter's Insurance			
Landscaping			
Other:			
Other:			
Other:			

Living Expenses	Expected	Actual	Difference
Food /Groceries			
Childcare			
Care Note/Gas/Insurance			
Clothes/Shoes			
Handbags & Accessories			
Entertainment (movies, concerts, amusement parks, camping)			
Dining out			
Beauty (Hair, Nails, Pedi, Eyebrows)			
Other:			
Other:			
Other:			

Long Term Expenses	Expected	Actual	Difference
New Home fund			
Emergency fund			
Savings fund			
Vacation fund			
Holiday fund			
Wedding fund			
Splurge item fund			
Other:			
Other:			
Other:			

Total Monthly Income:

Total Monthly Expenses:

Savings (difference between expected and actual expenses):

Monthly Expense Tracker

Housing Expenses	Expected	Actual	Difference
Mortgage/Rent			
Utilities (cable, internet, streaming services)			
HOA Fees			
Renter's Insurance			
Landscaping			
Other:			
Other:			
Other:			

Living Expenses	Expected	Actual	Difference
Food /Groceries			
Childcare			
Care Note/Gas/Insurance			
Clothes/Shoes			
Handbags & Accessories			
Entertainment (movies, concerts, amusement parks, camping)			
Dining out			
Beauty (Hair, Nails, Pedi, Eyebrows)			
Other:			
Other:			
Other:			

Long Term Expenses	Expected	Actual	Difference
New Home fund			
Emergency fund			
Savings fund			
Vacation fund			
Holiday fund			
Wedding fund			
Splurge item fund			
Other:			
Other:			
Other:			

Total Monthly Income:

Total Monthly Expenses:

Savings (difference between expected and actual expenses):

Monthly Expense Tracker

Housing Expenses	Expected	Actual	Difference
Mortgage/Rent			
Utilities (cable, internet, streaming services)			
HOA Fees			
Renter's Insurance			
Landscaping			
Other:			
Other:			
Other:			

Living Expenses	Expected	Actual	Difference
Food /Groceries			
Childcare			
Care Note/Gas/Insurance			
Clothes/Shoes			
Handbags & Accessories			
Entertainment (movies, concerts, amusement parks, camping)			
Dining out			
Beauty (Hair, Nails, Pedi, Eyebrows)			
Other:			
Other:			
Other:			

Long Term Expenses	Expected	Actual	Difference
New Home fund			
Emergency fund			
Savings fund			
Vacation fund			
Holiday fund			
Wedding fund			
Splurge item fund			
Other:			
Other:			
Other:			

Total Monthly Income:

Total Monthly Expenses:

Savings (difference between expected and actual expenses):

Monthly Expense Tracker

Housing Expenses	Expected	Actual	Difference
Mortgage/Rent			
Utilities (cable, internet, streaming services)			
HOA Fees			
Renter's Insurance			
Landscaping			
Other:			
Other:			
Other:			

Living Expenses	Expected	Actual	Difference
Food /Groceries			
Childcare			
Care Note/Gas/Insurance			
Clothes/Shoes			
Handbags & Accessories			
Entertainment (movies, concerts, amusement parks, camping)			
Dining out			
Beauty (Hair, Nails, Pedi, Eyebrows)			
Other:			
Other:			
Other:			

Long Term Expenses	Expected	Actual	Difference
New Home fund			
Emergency fund			
Savings fund			
Vacation fund			
Holiday fund			
Wedding fund			
Splurge item fund			
Other:			
Other:			
Other:			

Total Monthly Income:

Total Monthly Expenses:

Savings (difference between expected and actual expenses):

Monthly Expense Tracker

Housing Expenses	Expected	Actual	Difference
Mortgage/Rent			
Utilities (cable, internet, streaming services)			
HOA Fees			
Renter's Insurance			
Landscaping			
Other:			
Other:			
Other:			

Living Expenses	Expected	Actual	Difference
Food /Groceries			
Childcare			
Care Note/Gas/Insurance			
Clothes/Shoes			
Handbags & Accessories			
Entertainment (movies, concerts, amusement parks, camping)			
Dining out			
Beauty (Hair, Nails, Pedi, Eyebrows)			
Other:			
Other:			
Other:			

Long Term Expenses	Expected	Actual	Difference
New Home fund			
Emergency fund			
Savings fund			
Vacation fund			
Holiday fund			
Wedding fund			
Splurge item fund			
Other:			
Other:			
Other:			

Total Monthly Income:

Total Monthly Expenses:

Savings (difference between expected and actual expenses):

Monthly Expense Tracker

Housing Expenses	Expected	Actual	Difference
Mortgage/Rent			
Utilities (cable, internet, streaming services)			
HOA Fees			
Renter's Insurance			
Landscaping			
Other:			
Other:			
Other:			
Living Expenses	**Expected**	**Actual**	**Difference**
Food /Groceries			
Childcare			
Care Note/Gas/Insurance			
Clothes/Shoes			
Handbags & Accessories			
Entertainment (movies, concerts, amusement parks, camping)			
Dining out			
Beauty (Hair, Nails, Pedi, Eyebrows)			
Other:			
Other:			
Other:			
Long Term Expenses	**Expected**	**Actual**	**Difference**
New Home fund			
Emergency fund			
Savings fund			
Vacation fund			
Holiday fund			
Wedding fund			
Splurge item fund			
Other:			
Other:			
Other:			

Total Monthly Income:

Total Monthly Expenses:

Savings (difference between expected and actual expenses):

Monthly Expense Tracker

Housing Expenses	Expected	Actual	Difference
Mortgage/Rent			
Utilities (cable, internet, streaming services)			
HOA Fees			
Renter's Insurance			
Landscaping			
Other:			
Other:			
Other:			

Living Expenses	Expected	Actual	Difference
Food /Groceries			
Childcare			
Care Note/Gas/Insurance			
Clothes/Shoes			
Handbags & Accessories			
Entertainment (movies, concerts, amusement parks, camping)			
Dining out			
Beauty (Hair, Nails, Pedi, Eyebrows)			
Other:			
Other:			
Other:			

Long Term Expenses	Expected	Actual	Difference
New Home fund			
Emergency fund			
Savings fund			
Vacation fund			
Holiday fund			
Wedding fund			
Splurge item fund			
Other:			
Other:			
Other:			

Total Monthly Income:

Total Monthly Expenses:

Savings (difference between expected and actual expenses):

Monthly Expense Tracker

Housing Expenses	Expected	Actual	Difference
Mortgage/Rent			
Utilities (cable, internet, streaming services)			
HOA Fees			
Renter's Insurance			
Landscaping			
Other:			
Other:			
Other:			
Living Expenses	**Expected**	**Actual**	**Difference**
Food /Groceries			
Childcare			
Care Note/Gas/Insurance			
Clothes/Shoes			
Handbags & Accessories			
Entertainment (movies, concerts, amusement parks, camping)			
Dining out			
Beauty (Hair, Nails, Pedi, Eyebrows)			
Other:			
Other:			
Other:			
Long Term Expenses	**Expected**	**Actual**	**Difference**
New Home fund			
Emergency fund			
Savings fund			
Vacation fund			
Holiday fund			
Wedding fund			
Splurge item fund			
Other:			
Other:			
Other:			

Total Monthly Income:

Total Monthly Expenses:

Savings (difference between expected and actual expenses):

Monthly Expense Tracker

Housing Expenses	Expected	Actual	Difference
Mortgage/Rent			
Utilities (cable, internet, streaming services)			
HOA Fees			
Renter's Insurance			
Landscaping			
Other:			
Other:			
Other:			
Living Expenses	**Expected**	**Actual**	**Difference**
Food /Groceries			
Childcare			
Care Note/Gas/Insurance			
Clothes/Shoes			
Handbags & Accessories			
Entertainment (movies, concerts, amusement parks, camping)			
Dining out			
Beauty (Hair, Nails, Pedi, Eyebrows)			
Other:			
Other:			
Other:			
Long Term Expenses	**Expected**	**Actual**	**Difference**
New Home fund			
Emergency fund			
Savings fund			
Vacation fund			
Holiday fund			
Wedding fund			
Splurge item fund			
Other:			
Other:			
Other:			

Total Monthly Income:

Total Monthly Expenses:

Savings (difference between expected and actual expenses):

Monthly Expense Tracker

Housing Expenses	Expected	Actual	Difference
Mortgage/Rent			
Utilities (cable, internet, streaming services)			
HOA Fees			
Renter's Insurance			
Landscaping			
Other:			
Other:			
Other:			

Living Expenses	Expected	Actual	Difference
Food /Groceries			
Childcare			
Care Note/Gas/Insurance			
Clothes/Shoes			
Handbags & Accessories			
Entertainment (movies, concerts, amusement parks, camping)			
Dining out			
Beauty (Hair, Nails, Pedi, Eyebrows)			
Other:			
Other:			
Other:			

Long Term Expenses	Expected	Actual	Difference
New Home fund			
Emergency fund			
Savings fund			
Vacation fund			
Holiday fund			
Wedding fund			
Splurge item fund			
Other:			
Other:			
Other:			

Total Monthly Income:

Total Monthly Expenses:

Savings (difference between expected and actual expenses):

Monthly Expense Tracker

Housing Expenses	Expected	Actual	Difference
Mortgage/Rent			
Utilities (cable, internet, streaming services)			
HOA Fees			
Renter's Insurance			
Landscaping			
Other:			
Other:			
Other:			

Living Expenses	Expected	Actual	Difference
Food /Groceries			
Childcare			
Care Note/Gas/Insurance			
Clothes/Shoes			
Handbags & Accessories			
Entertainment (movies, concerts, amusement parks, camping)			
Dining out			
Beauty (Hair, Nails, Pedi, Eyebrows)			
Other:			
Other:			
Other:			

Long Term Expenses	Expected	Actual	Difference
New Home fund			
Emergency fund			
Savings fund			
Vacation fund			
Holiday fund			
Wedding fund			
Splurge item fund			
Other:			
Other:			
Other:			

Total Monthly Income:

Total Monthly Expenses:

Savings (difference between expected and actual expenses):

Monthly Expense Tracker

Housing Expenses	Expected	Actual	Difference
Mortgage/Rent			
Utilities (cable, internet, streaming services)			
HOA Fees			
Renter's Insurance			
Landscaping			
Other:			
Other:			
Other:			
Living Expenses	**Expected**	**Actual**	**Difference**
Food /Groceries			
Childcare			
Care Note/Gas/Insurance			
Clothes/Shoes			
Handbags & Accessories			
Entertainment (movies, concerts, amusement parks, camping)			
Dining out			
Beauty (Hair, Nails, Pedi, Eyebrows)			
Other:			
Other:			
Other:			
Long Term Expenses	**Expected**	**Actual**	**Difference**
New Home fund			
Emergency fund			
Savings fund			
Vacation fund			
Holiday fund			
Wedding fund			
Splurge item fund			
Other:			
Other:			
Other:			

Total Monthly Income:

Total Monthly Expenses:

Savings (difference between expected and actual expenses):

Flights in Stilettos

Monthly Expense Tracker

Housing Expenses	Expected	Actual	Difference
Mortgage/Rent			
Utilities (cable, internet, streaming services)			
HOA Fees			
Renter's Insurance			
Landscaping			
Other:			
Other:			
Other:			

Living Expenses	Expected	Actual	Difference
Food /Groceries			
Childcare			
Care Note/Gas/Insurance			
Clothes/Shoes			
Handbags & Accessories			
Entertainment (movies, concerts, amusement parks, camping)			
Dining out			
Beauty (Hair, Nails, Pedi, Eyebrows)			
Other:			
Other:			
Other:			

Long Term Expenses	Expected	Actual	Difference
New Home fund			
Emergency fund			
Savings fund			
Vacation fund			
Holiday fund			
Wedding fund			
Splurge item fund			
Other:			
Other:			
Other:			

Total Monthly Income:

Total Monthly Expenses:

Savings (difference between expected and actual expenses):

Monthly Expense Tracker

Housing Expenses	Expected	Actual	Difference
Mortgage/Rent			
Utilities (cable, internet, streaming services)			
HOA Fees			
Renter's Insurance			
Landscaping			
Other:			
Other:			
Other:			

Living Expenses	Expected	Actual	Difference
Food /Groceries			
Childcare			
Care Note/Gas/Insurance			
Clothes/Shoes			
Handbags & Accessories			
Entertainment (movies, concerts, amusement parks, camping)			
Dining out			
Beauty (Hair, Nails, Pedi, Eyebrows)			
Other:			
Other:			
Other:			

Long Term Expenses	Expected	Actual	Difference
New Home fund			
Emergency fund			
Savings fund			
Vacation fund			
Holiday fund			
Wedding fund			
Splurge item fund			
Other:			
Other:			
Other:			

Total Monthly Income:

Total Monthly Expenses:

Savings (difference between expected and actual expenses):

Monthly Expense Tracker

Housing Expenses	Expected	Actual	Difference
Mortgage/Rent			
Utilities (cable, internet, streaming services)			
HOA Fees			
Renter's Insurance			
Landscaping			
Other:			
Other:			
Other:			
Living Expenses	**Expected**	**Actual**	**Difference**
Food /Groceries			
Childcare			
Care Note/Gas/Insurance			
Clothes/Shoes			
Handbags & Accessories			
Entertainment (movies, concerts, amusement parks, camping)			
Dining out			
Beauty (Hair, Nails, Pedi, Eyebrows)			
Other:			
Other:			
Other:			
Long Term Expenses	**Expected**	**Actual**	**Difference**
New Home fund			
Emergency fund			
Savings fund			
Vacation fund			
Holiday fund			
Wedding fund			
Splurge item fund			
Other:			
Other:			
Other:			

Total Monthly Income:

Total Monthly Expenses:

Savings (difference between expected and actual expenses):

NOW THAT YOU HAVE A BETTER UNDERSTANDING OF YOUR BUDGET AND HOW TO TRACK YOUR MONTHLY EXPENSES, ARE YOU READY TO SHOP? LET'S GO. YOU'VE EARNED IT!

OTHER GUIDED JOURNALS & DIARIES
— *by* —
KINYATTA E. GRAY

I Miss You...
Daily Writing Prompts for Reflection, Remembrance, and Spirit Renewal

Fashionista's Travel Diary
A Guided Travel Diary for Travel Planning & Reflections

I'm Doing Me
The Ultimate Breakup Diary for Venting, Reflection & Spirit Renewal

While I'm Still Here
A Guided Expression Journal of Life, Love and Legacy for Those Preparing to Transition

My Crazy Teenage Life
The Ultimate Expression Diary for Venting, Self-Reflections and Self-Love

I Am A Man. I Have Feelings.
A Guided 90-Day Self-Reflections & Gratitude Journal for Men

The Queen's Manifestation Journal
Daily Writing Prompt for Manifesting the Life You Want

Kinyatta E. Gray is a Best-Selling Author, Travel Influencer and the CEO of FlightsInStilettos, LLC. Kinyatta is also the Chief Beach Towel Designer for the FlightsInStilettos Glam Girl Beach Towels.

Websites:

https://www.flightsinstilettos.com/

https://www.kinyattagray.com/

https://www.honoringmissbee.com/

Disclaimer:
Kinyatta Gray is not a financial management professional and is providing this information based on her personal experiences. If you are experiencing a financial crisis, seek the help of a certified financial professional.

www.ingramcontent.com/pod-product-compliance
Lightning Source LLC
Chambersburg PA
CBHW072018290426
44109CB00018B/2280